TRUE TALES OF YOUNG BRIDES

RELA KADIAM

Made with ♥ on the Notion Press Platform
www.notionpress.com

To my grandmother.

Contents

Preface

As a small child, I have always had strong, unbreakable opinions. One of these beliefs is that if a woman is not educated, she should not be married off at the brink of maturity. As I grew up and came to know about the horrors of reality, I discovered that the situation I had hated was called "child marriage"—the act of marrying off a child at a young age.

So, you can only imagine my reaction when I discovered that my grandmother was married off at the age of sixteen. I was shocked not only to hear the age at which she got married but also to learn that one of her sisters was married off at a much younger age than her. Her older sister was married at eleven. Eleven, now let that sink in. The age when you play with your friends, try to skip school by faking a stomach ache, celebrate birthday parties, and sleep on your mother's lap—a time of carefree days and bliss.

I found it so awful—the reality of this practice. But what was even more appalling to me was that this was always a custom the brides accepted. Through a quick search, I discovered many things I was unaware of. Regardless of child marriage being termed an offense in India since the year 1929, once solemnized and therefore officiated, the marriage is considered valid.

Reflecting on these facts brought to light the contrast between the legal aspect and lived realities. My grandmother's life, for instance, exemplified the personal toll of such customs.

My grandmother's life revolved around other people. When she was a child, her parents and siblings were her world. Once she turned sixteen, her husband soon took a place in her world. A year later, her children took the remaining attention. Something that I took note of through every conversation we had was that she had yet to really talk about herself. That may sound like an understatement, but to put it simply, it's not.

Through this book, I ultimately want to shed some light on these experiences—these little stories that may have seemed irrelevant to them. You might perhaps be thinking—what will a short book like this even do?

To answer this question, I think of this book as an internal fulfillment or an answer to my dissatisfaction. I think of it as a tribute to the child brides spread across the globe, but more so, my grandmother.

A Socio-Historical Context

Before delving into the stories of the child brides, I would like to set the stage by explaining the socio-historical context behind child marriage. Before diving into such a heavy topic, it's essential to build a prior understanding to truly grasp the events in each story.

The issue of child marriage is associated with a number of socio-cultural and historical contextual factors. It is not just a practice found in some regions of our world but a worldwide phenomenon beyond geographical borders. However, this book will focus on child marriage in India. This is because the problem of child marriage in India is a complicated one—influenced by deep historical roots, socio-economic factors, gender inequality, educational barriers, legal and regulatory challenges, regional variations, social pressure, health and safety concerns, religious and cultural beliefs, and—therefore, cannot be summed up in a single paragraph.

The Term 'Child Marriage'

Marriage is defined as a formalized relationship with legal standing between a male and a female, wherein sexual relations are legitimized. It is a religious and emotional union and bonding between two consenting individuals. In today's time, one would expect such a relationship to be between two consenting adults (individuals above the age of eighteen).

The idea of a child partaking in such a practice is, quite frankly, disturbing. This is not only because children cannot comprehend the nature and consequences of marriage but also because of how a child would concur with the traditional responsibilities required in matrimony. Can we really declare 'child marriage' a legitimate thing?

In simple terms, child marriage is a phenomenon in which a child is married off before the age of 18. The term 'child marriage' was constructed for a number of reasons. Firstly, to point out the utter paradox or contradiction that a child is equipped to participate in a marriage. Another reason for this is that a girl below the age of eighteen years is treated as a 'child' according to the Child Marriage Restraint Act (CMRA). The Indian Majority Act (1875) also defines the age of majority as eighteen years for the purpose of civil matters. Hence, in the context of India, 'child marriage' is the most appropriate term.

Focusing on The Girl Child

While researching and finally deciding that my main focus in the context of child marriage would be on the female child bride, I was asked a number of times—why? "Why only focus on the child bride? Don't child grooms exist as well?" The answer is yes, of course. Child marriage violates many of the fundamental rights of children. However, due to socio-economic factors and cultural beliefs surrounding purity and virginity, girls are more frequently subjected to early marriage. This disparity underscores broader gender inequalities, where traditional norms often devalue girls compared to boys.

Risks

It's no surprise that the timing of the marriage is an essential determinant of the woman's reproductive behavior. Child marriage typically causes quick conception of a fetus; thus, child-bearing is much more accessible and less 'time-consuming.' Scientifically speaking, a woman's peak reproductive years are between the late teens and late 20s. However, we must recognize that pregnancies at a young age pose significant health risks for young women, such as eclampsia, puerperal endometritis, and systemic infections ("Adolescent Pregnancy | WHO"). Miscarriages and stillbirths are also more common among young mothers. These risks are augmented by the living conditions of the woman, such as the possibility of living in poverty, malnutrition, and inadequate access to maternal and child health care services.

The Legal History of Child Marriage in India

Efforts for the legal prevention of child marriages began in the year 1880, starting with the change of the age of consent for the offense of rape. The change was intended to give protection to young girls from sexual abuse within the marriage boundaries.

Law Relating to Child Marriage

The Child Marriage Restraint Act (CMRA), enacted in 1929, was subsequently modified in 1949 and 1978 to increase the age of marriage, but the objectives of the amendments varied each time. Rather than focusing on the boundaries of sexual considerations, the changing CMRA concentrates on what is the appropriate age for a husband to have sexual relations with his wife. At the end of the day, her consent was deemed irrelevant since her parents were thought to be 'better equipped' and 'more educated' than a little girl to handle the question of her safety.

The Rukhmabai Case

The Rukhmabai Case was memorable for several reasons, primarily because it pitted the colonial state of British India against the multi-layered realm of Hindu law.

Rukhambai was married in 1874 when she was eleven years old. In 1884, her husband, Dadaji, had asked Rukhambai to stay with him. Defying his call, she refused to stay with him. Following this, Dadaji petitioned against her for the restitution of conjugal rights. In opposition, Rukhambai pleaded, saying that Dadaji was not entitled to the decree of restitution of conjugal rights on the grounds of social, economic, and personal incompatibility. This causated a proposition that a marriage must not be binding on a spouse who had not consented to it (Sagade 39).

Justice Pinhey perceived the marriage from a purely contractual basis. In his perspective, the parties' explicit consent was required for the marriage to be valid. However, in opposition, it was argued that Hindu marriage was a sacrament—meaning it was eternal. Introducing the requirement of consent in Indian marriages would render all (at the time) current marriages invalid and the children produced out of the union as illegitimate. It also welcomed a new door to improper alliances and the ultimate breakdown of social hierarchy.

And just as one would predict, the decision provoked immediate public chaos. For a minority, the decision represented a bold declaration for the rights of Indian women to personal freedom. For others, it was a 'slap in the face' to the piety of Hindu marriage.

The Phulmonee Case and the Age of Consent

The Phulmonee Case was a disturbing case that eventually garnered public support for the Age of Consent Bill.

Phulmonee, an eleven-year-old girl, had died from hemorrhage and vagina rapture—which was caused by being forcibly raped by her husband at the time. He was charged with murder, but the court exonerated him of the charge as Phulmonee was over ten years old.

Phulmonee's case highlighted the then-existing inadequacies of the law and eventually led to an amendment in the law of rape. The age of consent in 375 of the IPC was raised to twelve years in 1891. Subsequently, it was raised to thirteen in 1925 and fifteen in 1949.

Child Marriage Restraint Act, 1929

Popularly known as the 'Sarda Act,' The Child Marriage Restraint Act (CMRA) was established to 'eradicate the evil of child marriage.' This act, named after its sponsor Harbilas Sarda, a judge and member of Arya Samaj, initially fixed the age of marriage at 14 years for girls and 18 years for boys. It applied to British India, with the Princely states exempted from its purview. The Sarda Act was later amended in 1978, raising the legal marriage age to 18 for girls and 21 for boys.

However, although it marked a significant victory for the women's movement, the Act largely failed in practice. Only 167 out of 473 prosecutions were successful throughout its 2 years of enforcement.

Child Marriage in India—In the 21ˢᵗ Century

Two of the five stories I will be discussing bring to light the current role of child marriage in modern Indian society. These narratives show the ongoing impact surrounding this issue today, despite legal barriers such as the Prohibition of Child Marriage Act of 2006. They also reflect broader statistics indicating that, despite significant reductions in child marriage rates, approximately 1.5 million girls under 18 are married each year in India ("Child Marriage | UNICEF").

Child marriage is a global issue with complex socio-cultural and historical factors, but it is particularly intricate in India due to its deep-rooted historical, socio-economic, and cultural influences. After reading this, I hope you have gained a foundational understanding of the origins of child marriage in India.

CHAPTER TWO

The Goat Whisperer

When I first encountered Saanjh, the first things I noticed were the cheerfulness in her voice, her unbreakable smile, and her untouched innocence—yet I detected a faint hint of suffering in her body language. Despite that slight uneasiness, I continued with the interview. But, I soon realized that no individual is that easy to read at first sight. People are not codes; it's impossible to decipher a human being's train of thought, past, and true persona. Humans are designed to be implausibly complex, so there's no such thing as being able to read someone perfectly.

Once I finally had the opportunity to ask her questions about her early to later childhood, the slight hint of pain I first detected was unraveled almost instantly. It was as if I had reached parts of her soul that she was trying to conceal deep inside her. Saanjh was the very first person I interviewed, which I believe makes her the most memorable interviewee. At times, I observed, she seemed to soften her answers to make her experiences appear less lamentable than they actually were.

Many, if not all, of the women in Saanjh's family and community are child brides. When I discovered this fact, I was baffled. I knew child marriage was still prevalent in this day and age, but *actually* meeting a child bride who was married in the 21st century—and a recent one at that, as she was married only five years ago—made me sit down and ponder. The Prohibition Of Child Marriage (Amendment) Bill sought to raise the legal age of marriage for Indian women from 18 to 21 years and was sent to a parliamentary standing committee. The Bill sought to eradicate child marriage and bring about parity in the marriageable age for men and women. Legally speaking, a marriage in which either the girl is below 18 years of age or the boy is below 21 years of age is considered child marriage. Yet, Saanjh had been married at fifteen years old.

Through secondary research on Child Marriage in India via scholarly books, my understanding of the issue strengthened. Ultimately, I sought to answer my recurring question: How can a girl child in India be married before the age of 18, knowing that the Child Marriage Restraint Act exists?

According to S Chaudhary, "in early understandings–in both Hindu and Christian legal systems–marriage was a sacrament reflecting on unalterable divine will, rather than a social contract to be underwritten by the state."

To elaborate futher, to many rural folk like Saanjh, marriage is a sacrament, not a social contract. Technically speaking, she was not legally married to her husband at fifteen; she was religiously married to him. A religious marriage is defined as a marriage solemnized under any religious institute in accordance with the rites and ceremonies of any religious denomination. Legally, she may not have been married at 15, but socially and religiously, she was married at that age.

Saanjh was born and spent her early years in the small village of Mokila, Telangana, located on the outskirts of the capital city, Hyderabad. Mokila's landscape resembles that of many small villages in Telangana—lush, green farmlands. The lands in Mokila are abundantly fertile and expansive, stretching across several hundred acres of green woods.

Saanjh went to school until she was six. Unlike typical elementary school children, her early school days were neither simple nor burden-free. Every morning, she would walk a kilometer from home to school, and every evening, she would return home. Upon arriving home, she was expected to take care of the family's cattle. At first, Saanjh liked caring for the family's small herd of goats. However, over time, due to the amount of time needed for the goats, she missed many days of school just to watch the goats and ensure they were not stolen. Additionally, the goats had to be milked at least twice a day and were required to be washed once a week. Caring for the goats was a significant responsibility for Saanjh.

Over time, the goats became her younger siblings because, growing up in a household with three older sisters and four older brothers, Saanjh was the 'runt of the litter.' All three of her sisters were married off, while her brothers were living in different cities for better work opportunities. That meant that she was the only child living at home.

Things changed when Saanjh turned six years old. In the middle of first grade, her mother pulled her out of school. That year, her oldest brother, along with his wife and two kids, had moved to Pune, Maharashtra. Saanjh's mother insisted Saanjh tag along so she could take care of the two children while her brother worked. Little Saanjh, being only six years old at the time and having no say in the situation, was sent to Pune; this meant she was going to live six hundred kilometers away from home. Unlike the lush green of Mokila, Pune contained dry, deciduous forests and rocky grasslands. Pune was a foreign land to young

Saanjh—its people were different, the language they spoke was completely unfamiliar, and the city itself was like a maze to her.

I found it utterly baffling when Saanjh told me that, at the mere age of six, she fed, bathed, and cared for two children all day long. Despite being just a child herself, she was expected to take on the role of a nursemaid.

For two years, Saanjh lived in Pune, spending her days caring for her brother's home and his children. Her love for taking care of young children grew during that time. Saanjh had told me that those three years of her life were memorable, and she chose to bear the homesickness just because of her niece and nephew. Although I had emphasized that she herself was a child at the time, I assume the time she spent with her young agnates shaped her into the person she is today: gentle, kind, and considerate.

However, despite growing to enjoy caring for her nieces and nephews, Pune wasn't all that perfect. On numerous occasions, while Saanjh took care of the children, her sister-in-law would harass her. Day by day, her sister-in-law would yell at her on any and every occasion, and at times, the rude comments would even escalate to violent measures such as slapping, beating, and grabbing. Saanjh was merely a child, aged 6 to 8, when she endured those constant forms of abuse.

I remember much too vividly how she had burst into tears when she started talking about her sister-in-law's treatment. During the interview, I sat there in silence as she held back her sobs. The reason why she had never told her brother about her sister-in-law's violent actions was because she simply did not want to hurt her brother. She loved her brother too much to admit that his wife's actions were callous.

Once the children had grown up to an age where they no longer needed Saanjh to take care of them, Saanjh relocated back to Mokila, her hometown. After living in Pune for three years, she had grown accustomed to its different culture. But at the end of the day, nothing compared to the comfort of her home. At this point in her life, Saanjh was nine years old. Nine, meaning that it was finally her time to enter the real world. Her parents could no longer hold a steady income, considering their withering ages, so from then on, she began working.

Saanjh had told me that, in a way, there was never really a period of time in her life when she was not working. Even while she was attending school, she had been expected to care for the goats. Once she was removed from school, she was immediately moved to Pune, where she worked as her niece and nephew's caretaker. So, it was no surprise that once she arrived back home, she was expected to look for work.

Those jobs included cleaning the walls of a private school located in a close proximity to Mokila, cleaning the houses of economically well-off people, and working straining night shifts at a clothes factory. I was taken aback at the fact that she had been openly admitting that she was a victim, or rather an individual who had undergone child labor. This pushed me to research about the Child Labour (Prohibition and Regulation) Amendment Bill implemented in 2012. It stated that it prohibits the employment of adolescents (14-18 years) in hazardous occupations and processes.

It angered me that people knowlingly employed the young girl. But I also found myself challenging that opinion of mine. If Saanjh hadn't worked those hazardous and exhausting jobs, where would she and her family be now? Working was the only choice for her. It ensured her parents' safety and it put food on their plates. Education held no purpose in her life at the time; considering her situation, it consumed too much time and money that could have been used to maintain a stable household. So, what right did I have, as a privileged individual, to judge the decisions Saanjh was forced to make?

After discussing the working conditions Saanjh had faced in her various laborious jobs, I wanted to ask her the most important question: how did your marriage come about? To my surprise, Saanjh responded with a shy grin. At fifteen years old, Saanjh decided she wanted, or rather needed, to get married. She herself had asked her parents if she could marry.

I was still baffled by her early inclination to get married. I tried wrapping my mind around her actions and finally came to a conclusion: getting married was the only way she could escape financial instability. As much as one may argue against, marriage is considered somewhat of a social contract (even though I previously had pointed out how it is also considered a sacrament). In the long run, being married allows for a bond of interdependence between two individuals. Some may even call it symbiosis, where one organism depends on another for its own benefit. Saanjh may have thought like that.

On her wedding day, the burden of marriage finally sunk into Saanjh's mind. She had said that on her wedding day, she had come to a stage of pure regret. The words "am I too young for this?" circulated through Saanjh's mind. The question was valid, of course, and she knew that answer all too well.

CHAPTER THREE

The Gullible Little Girl

Imagine. You are eleven years old. Life is pretty easygoing. Your school days are full of chattering with your friends about the coolest movie stars. You forget to do your homework, so you try to convince your teacher otherwise, and during class, you attempt to pay attention but often end up mindlessly dozing into a deep slumber. Once the school day is over, you and your friends rush to a field to play games. When you finally tire of playing, you head home.

Dinner's ready on the table, so you quickly gobble up your portion before your mom scolds you. That night, as you get ready for bead, you and your sisters chit-chat about your future. All those dreams, aspirations, and yearnings may differ in some way or another, but one thing is for sure: marriage is not at the very top.

Shivani was like that. She didn't like school all that much. In her words, school was uninteresting and, well, boring. Instead of listening to endless lectures, she would much rather chat with her friends, play outside, or go to the movies with her sisters. She loved taking care of her little sisters. She loved her father dearly. She loved the comfort of her life.

Shivani is the older sister of my paternal grandmother, so I feel I know a lot more about her way of thinking and realize her overall in contrast to the other brides. Shivani's early childhood was a childhood filled with sweet, precious memories. Whenever I would ask her about that particular time in her life, her eyes would light up and a huge smile would spread across her face.

Shivani was born and raised in a city called Guntur, located in the South Indian state of Andhra Pradesh. Guntur is known for its chili, cotton, and tobacco exports. Its location is near the sea, so the climate is quite breezy. Shivani had lived in Guntur her whole life. Now reaching her mid-sixties, the place she has resided in her entire life has and will always be the place she calls home.

Shivani grew up in a large household consisting of seven daughters and two brothers. Therefore, a household with a majority of girls equated to a large burden—seven dowries. I wanted to know if Shivani ever minded this fact. I wanted to know if she minded how her mother had spent more time preparing food for the boys, how they had a separate eating time, and even a special ghee jar. She seemed confused at the sound of my question. I assume that the way her household worked was a default in her mind. It was a 'norm.'

One summer day, news arrived that her eldest sister had arranged to get married. Her eldest sister had been almost twenty at the time. Shivani and her sisters were overjoyed at this. Weddings meant an abundance of jewelry, sweets, decorations, and new dresses—so naturally, weddings were Shivani's favorite. A week prior to her sister's wedding day, her mother gifted her with a box of pure gold jewelry: shimmering, nifty pieces of various colored jewels encrusted into thick, golden spirals. Shivani had been utterly delighted at this. That day, she teasingly bragged to her little sisters about being gifted such beautiful pieces of jewelry. She didn't ask why she received such jewelry as well as a new, expensive dress. Perhaps it was a gift of goodwill from her mother.

The day of her sister's wedding had arrived in a hurry. The decorations had been set in place, guests were arriving, and music was playing loudly, yet something—just something—seemed off. Shivani noticed that she, out of all of her sisters, was being dressed with more attention.

An hour prior to the final ceremony, the *dandalu marpidi*, or in other words, when the bride and groom were to exchange garlands, Shivani's mother had instructed her to sit on the cushion next to her elder sister. Shivani didn't mind, of course; she thought that she could somehow provide her sister with some form of support. Shivani had obediently sat next to her sister, a wide grin across her face. She glanced at her sister and offered her a supportive smile while holding her hand with a comforting grip.

During the ceremony, the priest told Shivani to repeat the same sayings as her sisters. Shivani, who was raised to respect her elders, of course, obliged and followed her sister's actions. Paying no attention to the words, Shivani mindlessly whispered the prayers.

Following the ceremony, she hurriedly left to find her sisters. Little did eleven-year-old Shivani know that there was another man sitting next to her sister's groom. At eleven years old, Shivani had been religiously married to an adult man without her knowledge.

CHAPTER FOUR

The Daughter of the Mountain

I had never seen someone as vulnerable as my grandmother. I remember that day too vividly. I remember how she had sat on the bed, her back painfully arched, her legs flat, as she slowly rubbed her wounded leg over and over again. I watched her aged hand trying to soothe the pain in her leg. In reality, her leg wasn't the genuinely pained part of her—it was her heart. Rubbing her leg was her way of trying to soothe her internal pain and her heartache. Her eyes were red and puffy, and her mouth thinned into a line as she tried to hold back her sobs.

One week prior, she had undergone critical knee surgery. Four of her sisters had visited that day to aid her while she was recovering. One of those sisters was Shivani.

I never truly really realized how genuinely close those sisters were until I sat down and talked to them. Each one of those sisters looked distinctly different from the other. The oldest two, which included my grandmother, had light tan skin, wavy hair, and big, brown eyes. The youngest of the sisters shared the same dark skin, curly, shiny black hair, and bright smiles. Despite their physical differences, they all undoubtedly cherished their sweet childhood memories.

Just mentioning their childhood was something that brought grins to their faces. If you ask about their childhood home, they could go on talking, reminiscing for hours and hours. When the time came for my grandmother's sisters to leave, it was a long, emotional goodbye. They all burst into tears, circling around my grandmother, sharing kisses on the cheek and tight hugs. Their love for each other was unbreakable.

In Hindu mythology, the goddess Parvati was known as the "daughter of the mountain." She was the wife of Shiva, one of the main deities of Hinduism. Parvati's marriage to Shiva is considered one of the most divine unions; personally, I find it the most epic love story of all time. My grandmother was named after Parvati. Ironically, her marriage was far different from the divine romance she was named to honor.

My grandmother got married when she was sixteen years old. My grandfather was twenty-six. Unlike the goddess Parvati, who chose Shiva out of love and devotion, my grandmother had no say in her marriage.

I asked her how she came to know that she was to get wed, and she simply replied, "I overheard my parents talking about it." I asked her if they had asked her before for permission, and she simply shook her head and said, "Back then, you weren't able to decide if you wanted to get married or not."

My grandfather's mother had gone from house to house, village to village, town to town, all across the state, just to find a bride for her son. She had come down to Guntur to meet my grandmother's family when she came across my grandmother. I can only assume my grandmother's beauty impressed her as she went on to arrange for them to get married. The reason behind her hurriedly trying to get her son married was that they needed the money to get my great-aunt married. Using the dowry money bestowed upon them by my grandmother's family, they were able to later get my great-aunt married.

My grandmother and grandfather got married in Tirumala. A sour expression appeared on my grandmother's face when I asked her how that day had been. Apparently, the wedding was a hassle. According to her, her mother-in-law, my great-grandmother, had caused a ruckus because the event had been a mess. The musicians hadn't arrived on time, the food had apparently not been up to the mark, and the ceremony was out of order. My grandmother, being the sensitive girl she was, had burst into tears, overwhelmed by everything.

At sixteen years old, she was to live three hundred kilometers from her home. I wondered how considering the time frame of her marriage, it was practically impossible for her to communicate with her parents or siblings on a daily basis. She would have been terribly homesick. Even then, she told me with a grin on her face that her father had sent posts to her every so often to check up on her, asking how she was doing and how her days were going.

It took quite some time for my grandmother to adjust to the change of household. Her mother-in-law was growing frail to the point that she could no longer use her legs. This meant that my grandmother was the primary caregiver. It was a steep learning curve for a young girl who had grown up in a different environment.

My grandmother despised fish. Growing up in Guntur, her family very rarely ate dishes made with fish. But now that she was living in Nellore, a place located near the sea, her husband's family ate fish almost every day. And my grandmother hated it. I think at some point, considering the number of times she had to prepare the meals, the putrid fish odor became practically embedded into her nostrils.

Every day before dawn, she would go to the kitchen and soak rice and black gram. After draining the water, she would grind the two and then mix them together, letting them ferment. Following this, she would make idlis, a savory rice cake dish, for every single person in the household. Following breakfast, it was solely up to her to clean up after everyone. To this day, she remembers this routine with exhaustion. It was a time of immense duty, where her days blurred together in a ceaseless cycle of caregiving and household chores.

CHAPTER FIVE

The Pitiful Peony

At the age of eight, Amoli's father had been gruesomely murdered by a rival tribe residing in a neighboring *tanda* (tribal village). Over the course of one night, Amoli's whole life changed. His sudden death had left an eternal void, an unfixable crack in the family: a household of six people—four girls, a boy, and a single mother.

Amoli was forced to drop out of school from then on. To support the household financially, Amoli's older sisters started working on the farms of Mokila as day laborers. She on the other hand, was responsible for traveling to Hyderabad to work as a caretaker.

Similar to Saanjh, Amoli spent her early years taking care of young children in the city. Although the pay hadn't been a tidy sum, money was money, and the family needed it badly.

After reaching the age of twelve, It dawned on Amoli caretaking job simply did not make enough for the family. To fulfill the money they needed, Amoli picked up daily wage jobs such as gardening, cleaning, sweeping and dusting, painting the walls, and filling the cracks in buildings—anything that paid enough. The money she earned allowed her younger siblings to finish their schooling up to the twelfth grade.

The repetitive aspect of her life soon changed when Amoli fell in love with a local tanda boy. Amoli's eyes glistened, and she started giggling when she first mentioned her husband to me. She emphasized how their matrimony was a pure "love marriage"—one which is driven solely by the couple. Amoli had been fourteen years old and her husband had been eighteen years old. But that hadn't mattered to her because she really loved him. Soon, their romance was met by Amoli's mother-in-law's distaste. Due to the fact that Amoli had come from a poor family, her mother-in-law resented her deeply for the lack of dowry. I assumed their relationship was strong—a relationship founded on respect for each other—but I was very wrong.

Over the course of three years, following their marriage, Amoli's mother-in-law physically and mentally abused her. Her mother-in-law convinced her son that Amoli was a useless wife and a waste of money. This seemed to have worked because Amoli's husband soon grew to become physically violent. The beating became so threatening during a particular one-sided argument that Amoli faced brain damage due to the sheer impact inflicted on her head.

As a result, Amoli escaped to her mother's house to seek refuge from the violent tendencies of her husband and mother-in-law. During her story-telling, I prayed that this meant Amoli was no longer living with her husband and perhaps raising her children with the help of her siblings and mother.

Unfortunately, Amoli eventually returned to the dysfunctional duo. The reasoning behind this, I feel, is devistating. Perhaps it was due to societal expectations of a wife, or perhaps she felt a sense of responsibility. It's possible that she felt trapped in her circumstances, perhaps unable to see a way out. She ended up returning because her mother-in-law fell ill. She felt compelled to help her in her last days.

Even after enduring constant abuse, Amoli's sense of duty and compassion outweighed her own need for safety and peace.

CHAPTER SIX

The Daring Dreamer

Raadhi grew up in a small village located in Odisha, nearing the border between the states of Chattisgarh and Odisha. The province is known for its large mangos and glass-like rivers. From her description of her hometown, I can imagine the place to be like some sort of paradise. But once she described her family life, the picture of a haven disappeared almost instantly.

Like many other families in her village, Raadhi's family was very tight-knit and secretive. She grew up with all six of her cousins and her three siblings. Everyone, in brief, knew everything that was going on with each and every member of the family. Raadhi didn't mind that, of course, since it was the norm for her. But once she reached the age of maturity and self-awareness, problems started to arise because of the lack of privacy in her household.

Raadhi attended school until eighth grade, which is much higher compared to the other brides I talked to. She enjoyed going to school, mainly because she did better than her siblings. She liked how she could argue with her parents with logical reasoning from the things she learned at school. She enjoyed sitting at the front bench at school, trying to absorb any bit of knowledge she could; she was eager to turn her learning into a gateway to her dreams.

But, deep, deep down, she knew that school was not a permanent thing in her life. She knew she would eventually be taken out of school like her sisters. Raadhi's sisters were married at 12 and 13 to their second cousins. Both of Raadhi's sisters and their husbands lived in the same household as her, with their infant children. She knew she had no right to dream outside of the box she was born into; it was impossible to escape those closing walls.

When Raadhi turned 13, she met a boy named Udai. They became friends almost instantly, in her own words, she giggled, "we clicked instantly." They would spend school hours together laughing, playing, and just enjoying each other's company. Udai, according to Raadhi, wasn't like the other boys in Raadhi's village town. He was nice, respectful, and caring. He had moved all the way from Bhubaneswar, the capital city of Odisha so he was a "city boy" according to Raadhi.

At some point in their relationship, they became very close—which of course, caught the attention of Raadhi's parents. Her parents were furious. Raadhi's family threatened Raadhi that if she were to continue to interact with Udai, they would kill her. Raadhi didn't take her parent's remarks seriously and continued to hang out with the boy.

One morning, when Raadhi was dressed and ready to leave the house, she tried opening her bedroom door, but noticed that it was locked. Brushing off the possibility that she had been locked in her own house, she tried opening it once again. I wondered what Raadhi had felt when she realized the situation she was in. Did she think her parents were warning her, or was it their last straw? Did she think she would be locked in there forever?

At first, she tried knocking on the door gently, trying to appease her parents to seek pity on her. She had started to apologize, screaming "sorry" over and over again through the holes in her door.

Despite being in a household with a large number of people, not a single person had answered her pleas of mercy. At this point, Raadhi felt hopeless. She did not have a phone to contact any of her school friends or neighbors (not that they would have helped)—no one. She was helpless. Or in other words, utterly trapped.

Nightfall reached, and Raadhi hadn't eaten a thing. Tired, broken, and utterly depressed, she chose to sleep through what seemed to her an endless river of sorrow. She didn't hear a whisper from the house the entire day. Hitting her mental stopping point, she declared that she was too tired to care about what would happen to her tomorrow. Her hunger quickly turned numb, so she no longer complained or screamed for help.

A day or two had passed since her entrapment, and her parents had decided that enough time had passed. Raadhi discovered the door was no longer stuck; it was unlocked. She had flung her bedroom door open but hesitated before going downstairs. I feel that anyone would be absolutely terrified in a situation like this.

Her whole family was downstairs. Her parents, paternal grandparents, aunts, uncles, sisters, brothers, and cousins all sat down. Raadhi called out their names, sobbing.

Minutes of silence passed, and Raadhi's mother finally cracked as she said, "Raadhi. You are to be married today."

In that moment, it was as if Raadhi's entire world had come crashing down, leaving her dreams in ruins.

Conclusion

The topic of child marriage is highly complex. The women I interviewed came from diverse backgrounds. Three out of the five women were married in the 21st century. I included their stories to dispel the misconception that child marriage in India has been completely eradicated.

As privileged individuals, we often overlook this issue, dismissing it as a problem confined to the uneducated, the poor, and culturally distinct.

While all the stories I presented featured young brides, they differed in their thematic elements. Saanjh's story emphasized financial need, Shivani's highlighted consent, my grandmother's focused on duty, Amoli's dealt with control, and Raadhi's explored the sexuality of a girl child.

Thus, I believe it's important to contextualize child marriages within broader patriarchal ideologies such as gendered servitude, control over young girls' sexuality, and socio-economic factors like poverty. Simply focusing on raising the legal age of marriage won't suffice. My stories, I believe, illustrate a more complex reality than mere statistics convey.

Bibliography

A Study on Child Marriage in India: Situational Analysis in Three States. 2008.

"Adolescent Pregnancy." World Health Organization, Apr. 2024, https://www.who.int/news-room/fact-sheets/detail/adolescent-pregnancy.

Ahmed, Sufiya. Secrets of the Henna Girl. Penguin UK, 2012.

"An Epidemiological Study of Child Marriages in a Rural Community of Gujarat - PMC." PubMed Central (PMC), https://www.ncbi.nlm.nih.gov/pmc/articles/PMC4581144/.

"Child Marriage | UNICEF." UNICEF, https://www.unicef.org/protection/child-marriage.

"Government Releases List of States with Highest Percentage of Child Marriage, Jharkhand on Top - India Today." India Today, India Today, https://www.indiatoday.in/india/story/girl-child-marriage-high-percent-list-jharkhand-west-bengal-2282716-2022-10-08.

"Guideline for Child Marriage Eradication Scheme | Women & Child Development | Government Of Assam, India." Home | Women & Child Development | Government Of Assam, India, https://socialwelfare.assam.gov.in/documents-detail/guideline-for-child-marriage-eradication-scheme.

"Highest Child Marriage Prevalence Worldwide by Country | Statista." Statista, https://www.statista.com/statistics/1226532/countries-with-the-highest-child-marriage-rate/.

"How Is India Planning to End Child Marriage? - Civilsdaily." Civilsdaily, https://www.civilsdaily.com/news/child-marriage-india/.

"India Code: Prohibition of Child Marriage Act, 2006." India Code: Home, https://www.indiacode.nic.in/handle/123456789/2055?sam_handle=123456789/1362.

"Legal Age of Marriage in India: Govt Works to Raise Legal Age of Marriage for Women to 21 | India News - Times of India." The Times of India, Times of India, https://timesofindia.indiatimes.com/india/govt-works-to-raise-legal-age-of-marriage-for-women-to-21/articleshow/88328524.cms.

"Marriage Act: Women Empowerment & Child Development, Government Of Uttarakhand, India." Home: Women Empowerment & Child Development, Government Of Uttarakhand, India, https://wecd.uk.gov.in/pages/display/137-marriage-act.

Mascarenhas, Anuradha. "UN Programme to End Child Marriages Sees Progress in India, Looks to Promote Adolescent Rights in next Phase | Cities News,The Indian Express." The Indian Express, 2 Nov. 2022, https://indianexpress.com/article/cities/pune/un-programme-child-marriages-india-adolescent-rights-8245464/.

"Ministry of Women and Child Development: Measures to Prevent Child Marriages." Press Information Bureau, https://pib.gov.in/PressReleaseIframePage.aspx?PRID=1796829.

Mishra, Sneha. "Child Marriage in India (Amendment) Bill, 2021." Times of India Blog, 27 Sept. 2021, https://timesofindia.indiatimes.com/readersblog/myblogpower/child-marriage-in-india-amendment-bill-2021-37786/.

Modak, Purnendu. "Determinants of Girl-Child Marriage in High Prevalence States in IndiaPurnendu Modak." Journal of International Women's Studies.

Pande, Ishita. Sex, Law and the Politics of Age. Cambridge University Press, 2020.

Pathak, Sushmita, and Lauren Frayer. "Child Marriages Are Up In The Pandemic. Here's How India Tries To Stop Them." NPR, 2020, https://www.npr.org/sections/goatsandsoda/2020/11/05/931274119/child-marriages-are-up-in-the-pandemic-heres-how-india-tries-to-stop-them.

"Preventing Child Marriage in West Bengal: The Experience of Barddhaman District." Love, Labour and Law: Early and Child Marriage in India, SAGE Publications Pvt. Ltd, 2021, pp. 219–50, http://dx.doi.org/10.4135/9789354792915.n9.

Rao, Menaka. "More Education, Fewer Child Brides, Healthier Children." IndiaSpend: Data Journalism, Analysis on Indian Economy, Education, Healthcare, Agriculture, Politics, Indiaspend, 21 July 2017, https://www.indiaspend.com/more-education-fewer-child-brides-healthier-children-81262.

Sagade, Jaya, and Himalayan Club. Child Marriage in India. Oxford University Press, USA, 2005.

Sanghera, Jasvinder. Daughters of Shame. Hodder Paperbacks, 2009.

Shame. Hachette UK, 2007.

Sen, Samita, and Anindita Ghosh. Love, Labour and Law. Sage Publications Pvt. Limited, 2020.

"Steps Taken by Government to Prevent Child Marriages | Business Standard News." Business Standard, Business-Standard, 28 Apr. 2016, https://www.business-standard.com/article/government-press-release/steps-taken-by-government-to-prevent-child-marriages-116042801088_1.html.

"The Prohibition of Child Marriage (Amendment) Bill, 2021." PRS Legislative Research, https://prsindia.org/billtrack/the-prohibition-of-child-marriage-amendment-bill-2021.

www.ingramcontent.com/pod-product-compliance
Lightning Source LLC
Chambersburg PA
CBHW022124150726
47990CB00003B/1495